Every Day Worship

Carol Penner

MennoMedia
Harrisonburg, Virginia

MennoMedia
PO Box 866, Harrisonburg, Virginia 22803
www.MennoMedia.org

Every Day Worship
© 2018 by MennoMedia, Harrisonburg, Virginia 22803. 800-245-7894.
All rights reserved.
International Standard Book Number: 978-1-5138-0333-3
Printed in the United States of America
Design by Merrill Miller

All rights reserved. This publication may not be reproduced, stored in a
retrieval system, or transmitted in whole or in part, in any form, by any
means, electronic, mechanical, photocopying, recording, or otherwise
without prior permission of the copyright owners.

Unless otherwise noted, Scripture text is quoted, with permission,
from the *New Revised Standard Version*, © 1989, Division of Christian
Education of the National Council of Churches of Christ in the United
States of America and *The Message*, Copyright © 1993, 1994, 1995, 1996,
2000, 2001, 2002. Used by permission of NavPress Publishing Group.

Hymns referenced in this book are from *Hymnal: A Worship Book*
(Mennonite Publishing House; Faith & Life Press, 1992) and *Sing the
Journey* (Faith & Life Resources, 2005).

The content for this book was sponsored jointly by Mennonite Women
USA and Mennonite Women Canada.

22 21 20 19 18   10 9 8 7 6 5 4 3 2 1

CONTENTS

Introduction

IT'S HARD to describe worship. Worship is like coming home, or like entering the home of a beloved friend. I may have had a great day, or a rough day, but I open the door and someone is there whose presence is freedom. In worship we can just be silent, because we are known, or we can share anything we want.

Worship is also like the feeling I get when I'm swimming in a lake. I'm not a very good swimmer, so every once in a while I will put my foot down to check if the ground is there. Worship is like that motion, the reaching down to check that the ground is still there beneath our feet.

And worship is like the space between the stars when I'm looking up into the night sky with my friends. The dark is so deep and so wide that it opens up a channel right into my heart. Worship is the stretching we do when we encounter God's presence.

Those are three word pictures I've found to say what worship means for me. How would you describe worship?

For Christians, worshiping God is part and parcel of our life. It is in the rhythm of our days, our weeks, our years, our lives. It's something we do every day. Everyday worship defines our lives.

And yet, while worship is so central, so basic to who we are, we don't often talk about its purpose and its function. How do we describe it? How do we explain what it means in our lives?

I invite you to come with me as we explore Scripture and our faith through worship experiences. I'll be using the everyday parts of an average worship service to organize our study. Each chapter begins with a phrase that is commonly used in worship. Whether you are new to faith or have been a churchgoer all your life, we will unpack it together.

Along the way we will be praying together; we don't want to just talk about worship, we want to worship, and praying is a part of that.

I have written prayers for each of the sessions. Because of space limitations, you will find some of them on my worship blog, Leading in Worship (leadinginworship.com). I hope these prayers are starting points for you to say your own prayers. Feel free to add your own words and to pray in ways that fit your community.

Listen, can you hear? God is calling us to worship...

We are waiting for your presence, Lord—
patient as a lover sitting by the telephone,
    waiting for the voice of their beloved;
attentive as a farmer watching clouds for rain,
    waiting for the parched soil's relief;

intent as a child standing by the road,
    waiting for the parade to appear;
empty as a satellite dish scanning the heavens,
    waiting for a message from the stars;
poised as the still arms of a windmill,
    waiting for the wind's inspiration;
open as the wide sand beach,
    waiting for the tide's embrace.
Come, Lord Jesus!

—Carol Penner

How to use Every Day Worship

AS CHRISTIANS, we know about worship in our bones; we have been nurtured by our worshiping community. Scripture has shaped and is shaping our worshiping community. Scripture is itself a product of the worship life of the Jewish community and the early Christian church.

Each session in this study guide will help you reflect on Scripture in light of your personal worship practices and those of your congregation. Meditating on these biblical passages can deepen a specific part of your worship experience.

In each session, the Wonderings section provides some questions to help you flesh out how worship functions in your life. The final section of each session is action oriented. I encourage you to always include one activity when you meet together. We learn by doing, not just by talking.

Prayer is an essential part of this study guide. Some prayers are included in the session; other times you are given an online link to choose a prayer. These written prayers are not written in stone—feel free to modify and adapt them to fit your setting.

Some of the action suggestions are songs; when we sing we use our whole body in conversation with God. Feel free to substitute songs that are more familiar or appropriate to your community.

Women can use this guide in a variety of ways.

1. Individual reflection and group sharing. Women can read the lessons during the week at home, taking time to meditate on the biblical passages and reflecting on their own worship practices. When the group gathers, the time together is spent on the Wonderings section and the final action section, since everyone will have read the material themselves. This approach recognizes that group sharing is deeply enriched through time for personal reflection.

The role of the leader in this context is to facilitate sharing rather than to "teach" the lesson. The leader encourages each person to contribute to the communal learning process by sharing a story or insight from her own life that was brought to mind by the lesson. Sharing is facilitated if the leader is willing to show vulnerability by talking about how this applies to her own life. It may be that you will focus on one or two questions from the Wonderings section, to allow for depth of discussion.

2. A more traditional approach. For a more formal Bible study, you can read each section aloud, with readers for the biblical passages. When only one or two verses are cited, you may want to have these read in the context of the chapter. Questions for reflection might include:

How have you understood this passage in the past?

What is new or different about the ideas presented here, now that you are thinking of them in the context of worship?

What do you find interesting or intriguing?

What makes you uncomfortable?

What feelings do you notice as you reflect on this lesson?

How might the Spirit be inviting you to grow?

3. Personal devotions. It may be that you aren't part of a group that is studying *Every Day Worship*. As you read alone, this guide is best used when you give yourself plenty of time to reflect. Perhaps you want to read one section of each session per day. Allow the biblical passages to permeate your day; observe how the elements of worship function in your life specifically. Ask yourself:

Have I noticed this element of worship before?

How is it a part of my life, not just on Sunday, but every day?

Is this part of worship something that I have neglected or need in my life right now?

Being invitational

Christian worship should never be a space for just insiders. Our worship services are always open to newcomers; we want to share the good news! There will be a variety of people in every worship service: people who have worshiped in a Christian church their whole life, people who have just started to worship, and people who are attending worship for the first time.

Your group study could be the same. Do not assume that everyone has a long history with Christian worship. Some people may not have grown up in a Christian home, or even in a culture where Christianity is well known. It is important not to single people out, but rather to be invitational. Instead of saying, "What was worship like for you growing up?" say, "For those of you who attended church as a child, what was it like?" If people grew up in a different faith tradition entirely, ask them whether they are open to sharing how or if Christian practices resonate in some way with their own history.

Similarly, in any congregation, Christians can come from any denominational background. They will have different experiences that they can share. For example, you might ask, "If you attended church, how did you know the service was beginning; what happened?" Liturgical churches may begin the service with a procession or the ringing of bells; don't assume that everyone comes from an Anabaptist tradition.

Whatever the makeup of your group, pray for spiritual growth in an atmosphere of trust, confidentiality, and respect.

God is working in many different contexts and is calling on us to worship. *Every Day Worship* is an opportunity for us to share the rich pleasures of what happens in our community when we respond to that call.

ONE

Call to Worship

Come to me, all you that are weary and are carrying heavy burdens, and I will give you rest. Take my yoke upon you, and learn from me; for I am gentle and humble in heart, and you will find rest for your souls.
MATTHEW 11:28-29

We sit in this meeting house in quiet rows.
Our bodies carry our stories
even when we can't say them.
So many of us are bone-weary, or on the way to it.
Jesus, you know the heavy burdens we carry
day by day, and especially at night.
A yoke isn't exactly what we are looking for.
As we bow our heads to pray,
your gentle, scarred hands
lift something from us
with the quietest of movements.

You see the subtle shift of our shoulders,
the way they settle down,
like a child settling in its mother's arms,
relaxing under the weight
of her long, loving gaze.
Home, at last.

THE CALL TO WORSHIP is the doorway, the threshold. It might be someone going to a microphone and welcoming you to the Lord's house. Maybe it's Scripture and a responsive reading inviting you into God's presence. For some churches, the call to worship comes after a prelude, and in the silence after the music, words ring out. Come and worship!

Think of the call to worship as the moment when, arriving at a friend's house, the door opens and someone welcomes you warmly and ushers you in.

Some One Is Calling

Read the story of Moses and the burning bush in Exodus 3. Moses was probably having a hot, dusty day caring for the sheep. Was it curiosity, or was it the magnetic pull of an unseen force that drew him to the flaming bush? A voice he had never heard before spoke to him. He was on holy ground.

Recall together what happens in the rest of the story in the book of Exodus. How does God continue to reach out to the people of Israel? How do they respond when God calls them to dedicate their lives in a relationship of trust, of covenant?

This story of Moses and the burning bush reminds us that it is God who calls us to worship. It might not be as dramatic as a burning bush, but God is still drawing us to come close. The call to worship comes not just from a person. God is seeking us every day, and our response is worship.

Bow Down and Worship

The Hebrew word most commonly translated as worship is *shachah*. It means "to bow down" or "to prostrate oneself." We see the people of Israel bowing down before the pillar of cloud (Exodus 33:10). Moses bows his head when he is being instructed about the covenant (Exodus 34:8).

In Western customs today, the only time we might bow down is if we were to meet a member of a royal family. In Muslim services of prayer, people still bow down, face to the ground. For them, it's a posture of humbleness, honoring Allah.

In the Christian tradition, kneeling to pray is part of this bowing posture. The early Anabaptists in the 16th century knelt when they prayed.

The humility of a group bowing together was like a curtain opening for me.

As a child growing up in the Mennonite church, the only time I saw people kneel was when they were baptized. Our church had special communion services in the afternoon that only members attended. I was so surprised at my first communion when we were invited to kneel. People turned around and knelt at their pews, bowing their heads in prayer. There was the minister kneeling; there was Mr. Berg, the treasurer, kneeling; Mrs. Hildebrandt, my Sunday school teacher, kneeling; everyone on their knees. The humility of a group bowing together was like a curtain opening for me. I felt a Presence that I had not sensed before.

We see an echo of this posture every week if the worship leader asks us to bow our heads to pray. Together we have come into God's presence. The call to worship is an invitation to show humbleness before God.

Waiting for the Sun

At a lakeside town I know, many go to the beach to watch the sunset in summer. Some evenings the colors are spectacular, and the crowd claps appreciatively when the last brilliant sliver disappears. Worship is sometimes awesome like that—God is good!

But the beach crowd in that town comes even on overcast days. It looks like there will be a 0 percent chance of seeing the sunset, but people watch expectantly. That's like worship too. Some days we hope to feel God's presence, but it may not happen. Dark clouds rule the sky, and it just gets darker. Everyone turns and goes home.

But sometimes on those overcast days, just at the almost imperceptible crease between the sky and the lake, the sun explodes through like fireworks. Instantly, everything is illuminated! The water is incandescent, but sometimes only for a minute. Then it fades into gray ordinariness. Worship is like that too. The sudden illumination from God is all the more poignant for the fact that it's momentary, unpredictable, and totally out of our control.

In worship, sometimes we receive new insights into ourselves or the world. Sometimes bonds between our fellow church members are strengthened. Sometimes we feel the presence of God in a special way; an encounter with beauty or wholeness. And sometimes none of those things happen. Worship is simply our faithful response to God's call.

Wonderings

- Reflect on Moses's call. Can you think of a time God called you in a dramatic way to worship? Share with a partner, then with a group of four.

- In your congregation, what is the call to worship? How would a service be different if there were no call to worship?

- Share about a memorable worship service; why did it affect you deeply?

Let's Pray

Invite those who are able to choose a posture of prayer; it could be hands folded, or arms raised, or kneeling. Choose a call to worship that fits your group at "Prayers: Call to Worship" on *Leading in Worship* (http://carolpenner.typepad .com/leadinginworship/prayers-call-to-worship/).

Many songs are calls to worship; consider "Brethren, We Have Met to Worship" (*Hymnal: A Worship Book* #8).

TWO

Come to God's House

> *Surely the Lord is in this place—and I did not know it! . . .*
> *This is none other than the house of God, and this*
> *is the gate of heaven.*
> GENESIS 28:16-17

GOD COULDN'T have picked a more undeserving person than Jacob. Before you read the story of Jacob's dream in Genesis 28, skim through Genesis 27. Jacob is a liar and a cheat. He tricks his aging father and steals his brother Esau's blessing. And to top it all off, Jacob seems to have no remorse whatsoever. Esau is furious, and he is determined to have his revenge. Rebekah quickly bundles Jacob off to her relatives to save his life.

While running away from his own treachery, Jacob lies down to sleep, using a stone for a pillow. He has a dream about an angel-filled ladder reaching from earth to heaven. Jacob receives a message from God that he will be blessed with land and offspring. God promises not to leave Jacob.

When Jacob wakes, he realizes that he has been sleeping in a special place, a place that God has visited. He builds an altar, and calls that place *Beth-El* (Bethel in the NRSV), which means "house of God."

This story has captured the imagination of believers for centuries. When people built churches and cathedrals in the Middle Ages, Jacob and the ladder were often depicted in artwork as a visual reminder that there are holy places where we meet God.

God's presence comes as a gift. We encounter God not because we deserve it, but because God wills it. God is seeking us. We go to church to meet God, but God can find us anywhere.

Building God's House

When Moses comes down from Mount Sinai, he instructs the people that God wants a tabernacle, a place of worship (Exodus 26). The color of the tabernacle's curtains and even the clasps to hang them are described. Why so much detail?

The tabernacle was a symbol of God's kingship. The finest craftspeople contributed their gifts to create a beautiful home, a magnificent setting for worship. In order to honor their God, the people gave the best of what they had.

Throughout Christian history, church leaders used chapters like these to justify building magnificent houses of worship, filled with treasures and beauty.

Anabaptists in the 16th century rejected this approach. Jesus himself talked about destroying the temple (Mark

14:58). His body was the dwelling place for God that would be rebuilt. Because of this emphasis on Jesus, there was no longer a need for fancy places of worship. God's Spirit now dwells in the people of God (1 Corinthians 3:16-17).

Our Holy Places

Years ago, my four-year-old son accompanied us to the funeral of one of my uncles. It was in a Roman Catholic church. We entered the high-roofed sanctuary, which was dark and quiet. The only illumination was narrow beams of light streaming through blue stained glass windows. When we took our seats, my son leaned over and whispered to me, "This is a holy place."

I was surprised by his words. He had been in other churches, but he had never said anything like that about other buildings. The beauty of this sanctuary ushered him into holiness.

I was thinking of his comment last year when I was worshiping in the cathedral in Strasbourg, France. The space felt holy to me in exactly this same way. Yet I knew that the early Anabaptists had rejected the worship that was happening in this very building. They preferred to worship in homes and in the forest, in order to separate from what they saw as the abuses of the priests and the neglect of Scripture.

Once the persecution against the Anabaptists ended, they chose to build simple meetinghouses. They rejected representational art and fancy stained glassed windows. Rather than seeing these as aids to worship, they saw them all as roadblocks. This pattern of architectural choices continues today in most Mennonite churches.

I remember touring a Catholic friend through our Mennonite sanctuary. He was lost for words for a bit. He didn't want to offend me. Finally, he said, "It's very plain." I smiled. That was exactly it: that was the look Mennonites were going for.

Mennonites believe that places of worship become sacred when they are filled with faithful people praying in Jesus' name. The emphasis is on God's presence in the people gathered. Wherever Christians come together, it is a holy place, because God is there in our midst.

Holy Spaces

Although I love big cathedrals, the Mennonite sanctuaries I've worshiped in have been holy places for me. I recently visited the church where I grew up. I looked and saw where my father and stepmother walked on their wedding day. There was the pew where we sat to worship as a family. I sang with

Sanctuaries take on holiness. Our memories of honoring God there make them sacred places.

the choir in that choir loft by candlelight at Christmas. I knelt there to be baptized. That is where my father's casket stood. I was called to preach in that pulpit.

In a similar way, over time, our lives are filled with holiness because we remember God's presence in everyday experiences. Our homes could be called Beth-El. Our streets could be called Beth-El, our workplaces, our cities. God's presence makes the world a holy place, every single day.

Wonderings

- Share about a time when you, like Jacob, felt strongly that you were in Beth-El, the house of God.

- Discuss whether your worship meeting space is a sanctuary, a holy place for you.

- Is your worship space beautiful? How important is beauty in ushering you into worship?

- Sketch a church building you've visited that was a holy space for you. Or perhaps you have a photo of a church building on your phone. Share with the group.

Holy Spaces

If possible, have part of this session in your sanctuary. How does being in a traditionally "holy space" affect your discussion?

Share the "Sanctuary Prayer" from *Leading in Worship* (http://carolpenner.typepad.com/leadinginworship/2009/11/sanctuary-prayer.html).

Sing "What Is This Place" (*Hymnal: A Worship Book* #1).

THREE

Let's Worship Together!

For where two or three are gathered in my name,
I am there among them.
MATTHEW 18:20

READ MATTHEW 18 together. I think the whole chapter is summed up verse 20, and particularly in the phrase "I am there among them." Every part of the passage has to do with life in community. It's not easy living together, but God is with us in that struggle.

In today's Scripture, we see that God saves us together. This is similar to other Scriptures we've already studied. God doesn't just communicate with individuals like Moses or Jacob and say, "I will save you personally." God's message is for the people of Israel and for the whole world.

In the New Testament, Paul reminds his readers to spread Jesus' message of hope beyond their own group: "But you are a chosen race, a royal priesthood, a holy nation, God's own people, in order that you may proclaim the mighty acts of him who called you out of darkness into his marvelous light" (1 Peter 2:9).

Worship is not about me and my high and beautiful thoughts about God. It's about Jesus' followers meeting and being church together.

Church Shopping?

We recently moved to a new community, so I've been visiting churches. Some call that "church shopping." The problem with this term is that it can lead to a consumer mentality towards church. We want a congregation with these and these characteristics. Unfortunately, too often people today are church shoppers because they are church hoppers—they stay with one church for a few years and then move on.

It is hard to stay in one church for a long time. At first everyone is wonderful, but as time goes by, we get some history with people. We realize Mr. K is a jerk, and Ms. L is annoying. And then the M family with their pushy ways joins the church. That's the last straw! We start church shopping again.

But God is in the community, in the tension, in the learning to live together. We need to take Matthew 18 to heart and see community as a calling.

The writer of 1 John knows this: "Those who say, 'I love God,' and hate their brothers or sisters, are liars; for those who do not love a brother or sister whom they have seen, cannot love God whom they have not seen" (1 John 4:20).

This can be true in our study or small groups too. There are always people we wish wouldn't come. Being a Christian study group means learning to love each other, even when it is challenging.

Living with Diversity

The early church was diverse and was filled with conflict. Slaves and slave owners both attended. How do you worship together when one group is used to being served by people whom they think are inferior? Yet Paul never says, "Have one church for slave owners and one church for slaves."

In churches today, too often we are segregated. People who are richer go to this church; people who are poorer to that church. People with this color skin go here; those with that color go there. Many churches divide along lines of sexual orientation; lesbian and gay and transgender people are welcomed in this church, but not in that church.

Matthew 18 reminds us that there can be great tension in the community of faith, and that in such cases we should treat someone like a tax collector. How did Jesus treat tax collectors? He invited a tax collector to be one of his trusted friends!

Called to Community

I was not excited when God called me to be a pastor in a small inner-city church where the congregants were mostly very poor. I was solidly middle class and I didn't really know any people who were poor. They were different from me; I thought we would have little in common. To be honest, I would not have attended this church, except I was looking for a job, and they hired me. It's the sad truth, but there it is.

What I found was a group of people who loved me as I was. Their honesty, their refusal to pretend that things were okay, their willingness to go a second and third mile to help each other, was eye-opening.

I encountered a lot of diversity, and not just along economic lines. How would we help a visually impaired church member to lead worship? How could a person who had com-

Their honesty, their refusal to pretend that things were OK, their willingness to go a second and third mile to help each other, were eye opening.

mitted sexual offenses against children be loved and yet held accountable? What happens when families break down in front of your eyes? How can people held fast in chains of addiction break free? These are challenges you will find in any church, but often they are hidden. Here the challenges were transparent.

Was pastoring that church easy? Absolutely not. Some weeks were filled with conflict! But even when we had a tension-filled week, each Sunday we came together to worship. Worship demonstrated Jesus' power to break down dividing walls of hostility, even the walls that I built myself.

Mennonites have always believed that loving one another is central to being the church, but we haven't always been good at community. If you survey Mennonite history, we have often cast each other out of church instead of trying to live together. Worshiping God with the people God chooses for us is something we are still learning how to do.

Wonderings

- In pairs or groups of three, describe a difficult experience in the church. What led you to stay, even if it was hard?

- How is your study group diverse? In what ways do you celebrate that, and learn from each other?

- Can you think of a time when God helped make your congregation stronger by helping you work through conflict and tension?

Including Each One

Make a point of having the group greet each person by name: "(*Name*), you are welcome here."

Have individuals create a figure out of clay that represents themselves. Decide together how to place them in an arrangement that models church.

Share the "Social Fabric Prayer" from *Leading in Worship* (http://carolpenner.typepad.com/leadinginworship/2017/05/social-fabric-prayer.html).

FOUR

Time for Worship

Therefore the Israelites shall keep the sabbath,
observing the sabbath throughout their generations,
as a perpetual covenant.
EXODUS 31:16

FOR THOSE OF YOU who have grown up in the Christian tradition, describe what you know about what should happen on a Sabbath day. Then read Exodus 31:12-17, which explains Sabbath.

When I studied this text carefully, I was surprised that there is no mention here of going to a religious service. Sabbath is about imitating God and resting, just as God rested.

Sabbath in most of the Hebrew Bible is about rest, because worship happened only at the temple. It was impossible to travel there every week. That was reserved for special worship days. Rest was the way that people honored God.

Eventually, the temple was destroyed by invading forces, and the people of Israel were taken into exile. There they built synagogues, sacred places to pray and study together. It became the custom to worship God there on the Sabbath, the day of rest.

Early Christians also dedicated one day to God, but unlike the Jewish tradition, it was not on the seventh day of the week. Some of the first documents of the early church outside of the New Testament record that Christians were getting together on "the Lord's Day." This was the first day of the week, the day that Jesus rose from the dead, the day of resurrection. This day was a workday, so it was not marked by rest so much as it was marked by worship.

Times of Celebration

In Exodus 23:14-17, we read how the people of Israel were given specific instructions about worship festivals. These festivals were reminders of God's faithfulness in their history. The festivals were grouped around the rhythm of life and the farming cycle of firstfruits and harvest.

Christians, too, have worship celebrations that remind us of God's love. Many of our special worship times commemorate events in Jesus' life: his birth, death, and resurrection. Some churches celebrate other events significant in the New Testament story, like Epiphany and Pentecost. Christians in North America celebrate Thanksgiving to remember God's harvest blessings.

Worship is also part of the rhythm of our bodily lives. When children are born in the church community, they are brought to worship to be dedicated. Some congregations have prayers for new teenagers. Making a public decision to follow Christ happens at baptism. Worship is a part of our wedding celebrations, and sometimes we pray together at special anniversaries. When we die, our bodies or our ashes are brought into the sanctuary for a final worship service. From birth to death, worship is in the rhythm of our everyday lives.

Worship Patterns

Sociologists observe that Christians in North America are attending worship less regularly. While believers 50 years ago would go to church for worship weekly, today's regular church attender might only make it to church two or three times a month.

One thought is that life is busy. Most families have both parents working outside the home, and there are lots of scheduled activities that occupy our time.

That might all be true. But people have always been busy. In fact, you could make a case that for many in North America, basic survival is less strenuous than it used to be. We have more leisure time than ever before. Yet we always seem to be busy. Do we find time to rest? Rest is also part of God's Sabbath call.

I think about my friend's family. He grew up on a busy fruit farm, and when the cherries were ready to pick, they needed to be picked. But his family rested and went to worship on Sunday, even though farmers around them would be working. Losing a day's picking might mean they lost the crop of cherries, especially if rain was in the forecast. They were willing to sacrifice for both regular church attendance and Sabbath rest.

Worshipful Habits

While regular attendance with a worship community is essential for Christians, it's not the only time we are called to worship. Worshiping the Lord with gladness isn't just about Sunday morning. It's about finding time to turn our attention to God every day.

Many people have regular worship with God three times a day, because they say grace before meals. Or they say prayers each morning and evening. These are worship habits that nourish a spirit of thankfulness.

Worshiping the Lord with gladness isn't just about Sunday morning. It's about finding time to turn our attention to God every day.

Sitting down with your Bible is a way we often characterize worship at home, but there are many ways to worship God every day. I live near a woodland trail, and I hike there regularly. I often pray while I walk, absorbing the beauty of the trees. I am quiet in the silence of the forest.

Worship can also be something we do along the way in our working day. When I am driving, I often listen to meditative music that turns my attention to God. Or I listen to audiobooks that put me in a worshipful frame of mind.

Our time is in God's hands. God created us, and God will welcome us home when we die. All the time in between that is a gift, the gift of life. Turning to God and consciously spending time worshiping God is a faithful response to the God who made us!

Wonderings

- Do you make a habit of resting on Sundays? How?

- When is it hard to find the time to come to worship?

- How is worship something that you incorporate into your everyday life? Make a group chart as you answer this.

- Discuss the decision of the family with the fruit farm to not pick cherries on Sunday. Can you relate?

Worship Practices

Display some symbols from different special worship times in your congregation. How do they remind us of God's faithfulness?

If you have a tradition of reciting a prayer at mealtimes, share it with the group. Share "Our Evening and Morning Prayer" from *Leading in Worship* (http://carolpenner .typepad.com/leadinginworship/2017/09/our-evening-and -morning-prayer.html).

Sing "Come, Now Is the Time to Worship" (*Sing the Journey* #9) or "I Was There to Hear Your Borning Cry" (*Sing the Journey* #89).

FIVE

Join Together in Song

Worship the Lord with gladness,
come into his presence with singing.
PSALM 100:2

Loving God, thank you that you are the Great Composer,
and that you invite us to join the choir!
Thank you for all the parts;
soprano, alto, tenor, bass.
Thank you for the children's part and the seniors' part,
thank you for the youth part and the part for middle-agers,
thank you for the crazy baby descant
that we all love to hear each Sunday morning.
We are singing your song today:
help us to sing true and clear,
listening for your voice in our ears,
hearing you in the voices all around us. Amen.

Being In Harmony with One Another

Read Psalm 100 together. David is the most famous of musicians in the Bible; his beautiful songs of praise to God have inspired worship for centuries. But David didn't invent the idea of music for worship. Moses sang with the people of Israel, and Miriam took up a tambourine to sing and praise God after they were delivered from Pharaoh's power (Exodus 15). A lesser known story of the power of music in worship is about the prophet Elisha (2 Kings 3:9-20).

Music and communing with God has a long history in the Jewish faith. Since the early church was at first largely made up of Jewish people, it is no surprise that singing was a regular part of worship (1 Corinthians 14:26).

Mennonites are famous for their tradition of choral hymn singing. I grew up in a big congregation that had a choir loft that held 60 people. Every Thursday evening, I would go to choir practice; our choir sang every Sunday. Even as children, we sang songs in Sunday school and were taught to sing in parts.

Mennonites around the world have rich, varied traditions of singing.

Music is an important part of worship for Mennonites, even if today we might not always sing hymns. Many churches project the words to songs on the wall, and no longer use hymnbooks. Today, harmonies may be provided for us by worship singers at the front, or by instrumentalists. Mennonites around the world have rich, varied traditions of singing.

Joining voices is a communal practice that psychologists have been studying. They have discovered that there are health benefits to singing! Breathing and harmonizing together reduces anxiety. As Christians, we see God's hand in this. The words of the African American spiritual sum it up as we sing: "Glory, glory, since I laid my burden down."

Making Melody in Our Hearts

The writer of the letter to the Ephesians is pessimistic about the world, saying, "The days are evil" (Ephesians 5:16). Sometimes I identify with that assessment, when I hear of another mass shooting, terrorist attack, or war. But the writer reminds us to be thankful, no matter what our context. We can still sing hymns with others and by ourselves, "making melody to the Lord" in our hearts (Ephesians 5:19).

I had a singing grandmother. My mother died when I was little, and as my grandmother raised us, she sang and sang. I learned to sing from her. I can't tell you how many times I've found myself humming some hymn, and when I think of the words of the tune, I realize they are exactly the message of hope I need.

I was a personal support worker in a nursing home for several years after high school. Every day I cared for Mrs. B, who had lost the ability to speak because of a stroke. Her husband visited regularly, but one evening I heard two people singing in her room. I wondered who else had come to visit. You can imagine my surprise when I saw it was Mrs. B singing with her husband. She had lost the ability to speak, but she could clearly sing all the words to the hymns she knew by heart. The part of the brain that creates music was not damaged by the stroke.

Music touches us in a different way than talking does. Singing to God, and singing together to God, shapes us as a people in deep and mysterious ways.

A Time for Silence

While making sounds for God is part of worship, silence has always been a faithful response to God as well. The prophet Habakkuk writes, "But the Lord is in his holy temple; let all the earth keep silence before him!" (Habakkuk 2:20).

Long periods of silence are not a characteristic of Mennonite worship; however, there are moments of silence. In my congregation, there is the moment of silence between the prelude and the beginning of the service. When we have a choir, there is the moment when the conductor stands before the waiting singers and we wait for the music to begin. We usually have a sharing time, and there is the silence while we wait to see whether people want to speak. These moments are all important; if you took them away and filled them up with sound, I think our service would suffer.

Silence allows God to bring thoughts and people to our attention without the distraction of sound.

Silence is extremely important for me in my life. I truly revel in the peacefulness of no sound. When I have been with a group of people all day, I thirst for silence like water. Silence allows God to bring thoughts and people to our attention without the distraction of sound. Silence also offers us the chance to shape our thoughts into prayer and to hear God's voice.

Wonderings

- Can you share a moment where music or a certain hymn helped you feel closer to God?

- Congregations worship with a variety of musical styles; share a song that you have come to love, even though it is very different from the music with which you grew up.

- Is silence something you seek or avoid?

Make Melody Together

Have a selection of hymnbooks displayed from different time periods in your church's life.

Sing "O Sing to the Lord" (*Sing the Journey* #12) and "Oh, for a Thousand Tongues to Sing" (*Hymnal: A Worship Book* #110). Let any musicians in your group know about the songs ahead of time, and invite them to bring instruments.

Share a prayer about music from "Music" on *Leading in Worship* (http://carolpenner.typepad.com/leadinginworship/music/).

SIX

Hear the Word of the Lord

Your word is a lamp to my feet and a light to my path.
PSALM 119:105

If you continue in my word, you are truly my disciples;
and you will know the truth, and the truth will
make you free.
JOHN 8:31-2

Living Word, thank you for giving us Scripture,
which is a lamp for our feet and a light for our path.
Thank you for all who wrote it, copied it,
died protecting it, translated it, and published it.
Thank you for the freedom to own and distribute Bibles,
which many people in this world do not have.
Thank you for the people who shared the Bible with us:

family members, Sunday school teachers, preachers.
Thank you that we can read it together and learn from it.
And having read it, help us live it!
Give us the courage to follow your path;
the path of truth, the path of freedom. Amen.

Devotion to the Word

Read Exodus 24:1-8. Moses is fresh from Mount Sinai, and he is eager to share what he has learned from God. Writing down the revelation from God and repeating it aloud to the gathered people becomes a model for worship that will be followed for centuries.

In Roman Catholic worship services in the 1500s, Scripture was read in Latin, which most of the people listening did not understand. Reformers believed that understanding Scripture was important, so they started translating it into the languages that people spoke. They campaigned to have these translations used in church. This resulted in persecution and death for many brave and courageous Christians.

At that time there was a huge appetite for Scripture. The invention of the printing press suddenly meant that people could afford to own a printed book. The Anabaptists read the Bible in their own language. They felt that there were differences between what they read in the New Testament and the structure of the churches they were worshiping in. They suggested reforms, but these were rejected. Anabaptists either left or were forced from established churches. They found that reading the Bible changed their lives in dramatic ways: it resulted in renewed faithfulness, and also in exile, torture, and even death. We read about these people in the book *Martyrs Mirror* by Thieleman J. van Braght.

Reading Together

In Luke 4:16-30 we see Jesus reading Scripture out loud. This story is a window into Jewish worship practices. Gathering in a synagogue and reading Scripture and studying it together was a common Jewish practice. In the Luke text, once Jesus finishes reading, they look at him, because they expect him to discuss or explain what he has read.

We see this same pattern in Acts 17:1-3, when Paul and Silas arrive in Thessalonica. They go to the synagogue and explain how the Scriptures point to Jesus.

Christian worship followed this Jewish tradition and has always included Scripture reading accompanied by someone explaining or discussing it. We call this preaching.

In the Mennonite tradition, preaching is not just the job of the leader or minister. Often, people from the congregation will take a turn at interpreting the Bible in a Sunday service. We believe that God's Spirit helps us understand the Bible best when we study together.

But Sunday is not the only time we do this. Studying Scripture at home, as well as in small group Bible studies, is a regular part of most Christian communities.

I remember gathering with other teenagers in my church to study the Bible. Sitting in a circle with our Bibles on our laps, we felt God's presence among us. I had sat in a circle in Sunday school classes since I was a child, but suddenly now the Bible seemed alive with meaning. We were eager to read it—something that hadn't always been the case when we were children, as our Sunday school teachers witnessed!

A Visible Word

Growing up in my grandmother's house, I saw Bible verses every day. She had several plaques inscribed with Bible verses on the walls. This was the case in other homes I visited. This is less fashionable today. I have a Scripture verse hanging in my office, but not in the rest of my house. My home is not unusual; most of my friends' homes are the same.

In Deuteronomy 6:6-9 the Israelites are instructed to put an important Scripture on the doorposts of their homes. They would see it every time they enter and exit. I wonder whether my grandmother got something right that we miss today.

Words are signposts, they are symbols, they are pointers to the living Word, who is Jesus Christ.

Of course, the words themselves are not divine. We don't worship words. Words are signposts, they are symbols, they are pointers to the living Word, who is Jesus Christ. Jesus is the Word who is written on our hearts.

I remember visiting someone who unexpectedly ended up in the intensive care unit of the hospital. His wife was frantic with worry. When I arrived, she asked if I had a Bible. She wanted to look for comfort, and she knew that the Bible was a place she could find it.

I know that in my own hard times, I have sometimes just copied out Scripture. Repeating the words, savoring them, learning them by heart, hearing the word of the Lord to me.

Wonderings

- Invite anyone who has a Bible that has special meaning to bring it and share a story about it.

- Share about a sermon series or Bible study that was significant in deepening your faith.

- If you needed comfort, what passage of Scripture would you choose to copy out by hand?

The Word in Your Hands

If your church has a Bible in the sanctuary or on the pulpit, place that Bible in the middle of your meeting space.

Have the Scripture reader stand to read Scripture, as a way of honoring the power of the text. Say "Thanks be to God" at the conclusion of the reading.

Sing "God of the Bible" (*Sing the Journey* #27). Are there other hymns or songs about Scripture that you can share?

SEVEN

Give Thanks to the Lord

And Ezra said: "You are the Lord, you alone; you have made
heaven, the heaven of heavens, with all their host, the earth
and all that is on it, the seas and all that is in them. To all of
them you give life, and the host of heaven worships you."
NEHEMIAH 9:6

Your call to thankfulness comes wrapped
in the poised dewdrop on the tip of the green leaf,
the world reflected upside down
in the perfect sphere of crystal light.
Your call beckons in the words spoken
from a book that reads our lives,
whispering promises new every day.
Your call enlivens us as we sing together,
our lungs filling with one purpose.

Thank you for your persistent invitation,
even when time after time, we're oblivious,
turning our attention instead
to every busyness under the sun.
But today, here, now, we lay ourselves open
to the gift of life abundant.
We give thanks.

Praying Together

Read 1 Thessalonians 5:12-28. Paul is writing to the church at Thessalonica, encouraging them in their faith. One of the things Paul suggests is that we can be thankful "in all circumstances" (v. 18). We may not be thankful *for* all things, but *in* all things, we can be thankful.

The Greek word for thankfulness here is *eucharisteo*. It is the same verb that describes Jesus' prayer when he broke the bread in the upper room with his disciples. He knew that the next day he would be crucified, yet he still gave thanks. Jesus modeled giving thanks in all circumstances.

How do we foster thankfulness in our lives? One of the ways we do this is that when we gather together as Christians, we give thanks to God together.

As a pastor, I've had many opportunities to guide worship leaders as they prepare congregational prayers for worship services. I've found that most of their prayers are short on thankfulness and long on petitions. I encourage them to reverse that. If we want to be thankful people, we need to spend more of our prayer time talking about thankfulness.

Holy Attention

I think the most effective prayers are very specific. Using your eyes, your ears, your nose, your sense of touch and taste, what did you experience this week that was wonderful? Instead of praying, "Thank you, God, for food," can we make our prayers more concrete? Perhaps it was fresh food from the garden: "Thank you for the fresh taste of spring, for strawberries, red and juicy, sweet and tangy on our tongues!" By naming precisely what we are thankful for, we pay attention to the gifts that God gives us.

As people of God, we want to encourage each other to become more thankful.

As people of God, we want to encourage each other to become more thankful. This isn't accomplished by lecturing each other on the benefits of being thankful. This is accomplished by paying close attention to the attitudes we ourselves have in our day-to-day lives.

I know one family that has a regular topic for dinner conversation. The question is, "What is the best thing that happened to you today?" This helps to focus the family's attention on good things that can be celebrated together. They also ask the questions, later, "What was the worst or most challenging that happened to you today? How did you get through it?"

Can we find the discipline and spiritual strength to pay attention to the blessings that are showered on us each and every day? Can we model that for those around us? It's not about denying or ignoring that hard things happen, but about finding that even in the midst of the hardest times, God brings rich blessings.

Surprised by the Holy

There are times in our lives where the holy bowls us over. We fall to our knees or we open our arms wide. We bow our heads or lift our eyes to heaven. We are in the presence of something so big, so mysterious, and so wonderful that we don't even stop to think. Giving thanks is what we have to do.

For some it happens on the shores of a crystal-blue mountain lake. For others it's in the exhausted, sweat-laden moment when a new baby emerges and they hold it for the first time. And it happens in an everyday ordinary moment in an everyday ordinary place, where suddenly the extraordinariness of life and the world we live in is revealed in a tiny glimpse of insight, precious and lasting.

I recall a friend telling me about a hurried morning when everyone was running out the door. Waiting for his daughter to grab her backpack, the father paused in the driveway. Suddenly a sparrow landed on his shoulder. All at once, everything else dropped away. The sheer wonder of this, a little creature perched with light feet, chirruping softly, filled his attention. His daughter emerged, and she saw her father transfixed. Everyone joined in quiet wonder. After two minutes the bird hopped to my friend's head, and then flew away. The family smiled at each other, their day changed. They experienced the visit of the sparrow as a gift from God, a gift of deep peace.

Thankfulness and peace are deeply related: "And let the peace of Christ rule in your hearts, to which indeed you were called in the one body. And be thankful" (Colossians 3:15). When God's peace fills us, we are thankful people.

They experienced the visit of the sparrow as a gift from God, a gift of deep peace.

Wonderings

- In groups of two or three, reflect on a hard time in your life. Were there things to be thankful for even in difficult circumstances?

- Describe a sudden awareness of beauty that caused you to pause in the hustle and bustle of your daily life. How was God in that moment?

Being Thankful

Read Psalm 136 responsively.

Silently and slowly take a prayer walk together in your neighborhood or church building. Pay attention to what is around you, cultivating an openness to beauty. Come back and have a time of prayer in which you each name one thing for which you are thankful.

Sing "We Plow the Fields and Scatter" (*Hymnal: A Worship Book* #96) or "Long before My Journey's Start" (*Sing the Journey* #36).

EIGHT

Confess Our Sins

Therefore confess your sins to one another, and pray for one another, so that you may be healed. The prayer of the righteous is powerful and effective.

JAMES 5:16

The call to confess is the least popular call of all.
Can't we just have a call to ministry,
or a call to faith, or a call to prayer?
Confessing sins makes our skin crawl.
I can confess to you, God. Maybe.
In the privacy of my own room, in the dark.
But confessing to others would mean
having other people realize that I messed up;
letting people see that I have hurt someone.
People would hold me accountable.
They would ask me if I've made things right.
I don't know if I want them to have that power.

God, I confess that I hate confession,
and I hate confessing to others
more than I hate confessing to you.
Can we start there?

We Confess

Read Nehemiah 9:1-5. Confession of sins before God has a long tradition in the Jewish faith. Can you think of times in the Hebrew Bible where people or individuals confessed their sins? God established a covenant relationship with the people of Israel, but over and over again they failed to hold up their side of the bargain. In the Nehemiah passage, the people are returning from exile to rebuild the city of Jerusalem. They confess not only their own sins but the sins of their ancestors.

The writer of Proverbs reminds us that mercy comes after confession.

Confessing sins is an essential part of our relationship with God. The writer of Proverbs reminds us that mercy comes after confession (Proverbs 28:13). Confession is the way we show our repentance. It's an essential part of receiving forgiveness.

When my daughter was eight years old, she was playing with her brother at my husband's office while we did some work outside the building. We were surprised when two fire-trucks and an ambulance rolled up, lights flashing. We assured them there was no emergency, but they had received a 911 call from our number. We asked the children whether they had called 911. They were adamant that they had not. That evening my daughter went to bed early, saying, "I feel sick." In the dark in her room, she confessed to me that she had called 911, and had hung up immediately. She didn't know they could trace the call.

Childish mistakes can make us feel sick, but sin is a type of sickness in our soul. It poisons us; it needs to get out. Confession is a way that we ask God to forgive us, to cleanse us. John the Baptist called people to repentance, and before they were baptized, they confessed their sins (Matthew 3:1-6).

Confessing in Community

From the earliest church, confession has been a part of Christian worship services. In the Roman Catholic church, it became a practice that people would confess to their priest before receiving communion. The priest would counsel them about a practice of penance, which was a way of showing the seriousness of their confession. They might be required to return something they stole, apologize to someone they hurt, or say prayers to turn their soul to God.

In Mennonite churches today, there may or may not be a prayer of confession in a worship service. We may not like to concentrate on our sins very often. Perhaps we worry that it will make people feel bad about themselves. Our culture encourages us to build up people's self-esteem, not point out their flaws. Yet our consciences are a God-given part of us, and when we do something wrong, that sin can be a burden. Confession to God is an important pastoral service when we worship together.

One elderly woman told me that when she was young, before the twice-a-year communion service held on Sunday evenings, members would line up in the afternoon and talk to the pastor one by one to confess their sins. When someone took a long time in the pastor's office, people looked at each other, and wondered, "What are they confessing?"

Baptism is usually a time where we confess that we are sinners and publicly accept God's forgiveness. Remembering our sinfulness is an important practice of the Christian church; it helps us realize the significance of Christ's sacrifice for us on the cross.

Walking Together

We don't just sin as individuals. As groups and societies and nations, we make very big mistakes that have lasting consequences. Colonial European powers exploited the lands they conquered, sending untold wealth to Europe. People kidnapped and traded African peoples as slaves. White settlers coming to North America stole the land from Aboriginal peoples, and careless domination of creation has caused the extinction of thousands of species.

In the Nehemiah passage, the people apologize for the sins of their ancestors. Some still benefit from things that happened before they were born. I think of Mennonite settlers who came to Waterloo County in Ontario in the 1800s. They bought land that had been promised to the Attawandaron, Anishinaabe, and Haudenosaunee peoples. Today, white people still own most of this land, while the reserve for First Nations people is very small.

We live in a very complex world, and praying publicly about our own sins and the sins of our ancestors is a way of acknowledging that we need God's help in figuring out how to live justly with our neighbors.

Wonderings

- We talk about forgiveness in church, but do we talk enough about confession? Is confession a part of your worship services? Why or why not?

- If we never talk about what we have done wrong, what message does this send to newcomers about our community?

Confessing Our Sins

Print out several different confessional prayers. If you are in your church building, tape them around the sanctuary and invite people to take a confessional walk, praying each prayer silently. When you are finished, come back and talk about the experience of thinking about our sins. You can find some confessional prayers in *Hymnal: A Worship Book* (#690– #709) and at "Prayers: Confession" on *Leading in Worship* (http://carolpenner.typepad.com/leadinginworship/prayers -confession/).

NINE

Let's Pray to God

Ask, and it will be given you; search, and you will find;
knock, and the door will be opened for you.
MATTHEW 7:7

Creator, how can we describe to you the beauty of this
land?

Why does the dawn fill us with hope?

Can you move in us like this fresh wind,

clearing out cobwebs of complacency?

Jesus, why is there deep pain in our lives?

Can you give us courage to embrace those who are
hurting?

Holy Spirit, can your power heal the great rifts in our
world?

How are we to be agents for change when we ourselves
doubt your power?

Can you open our eyes to how you are already working
    for peace
in ways that we cannot fathom or understand?
God who created us, and walks with us,
can you hear our prayers even when they are only
    questions?

Teach Us to Pray

Read 2 Samuel 12:15-23. This is one of the more famous times that David prays for help. In the songs, or psalms, he wrote, we see a wide range of requests. When David is being pursued by his son Absalom, he asks for deliverance (Psalm 3). When he is sick with fear, he asks for deliverance (Psalm 6). He calls on God for judgment for people who are persecuting him (Psalm 7). He asks God to save him from the gates of death (Psalm 9).

But David's prayers are not just a list of requests. The Psalms are perhaps most known for their attitude of praise; they describe God's greatness.

I think that dedication to God is why David was "a man after [God's] own heart" (1 Samuel 13:14). It wasn't because David was such a moral man. In fact, he did a lot of very bad things. But Scripture does show David continually turning to God in prayer.

The Bible is full of stories about people who turn to God for help. God heard the people crying in Egypt and delivered them. And then there's Hannah, asking for a child, and Elijah praying for rain, to name a few. The Hebrew Scriptures teach that the people who follow God can count on God listening to and answering their prayers.

That's the tradition that Jesus grew up in. Jesus grew up learning to pray from his Jewish family and culture. He was taught how to pray not by a single person, but by a community modeling faithful prayer day by day, year by year.

Some people learn to pray at home, with their families. Others come from families that are not religious. We can learn to pray as members of a church community. Whenever we gather as Christians, prayer comes naturally. We pray in Sunday worship services, we pray in Sunday school classes and small groups. Prayer permeates our lives and we absorb the praying life, almost by osmosis.

Praying for the World

I have an older friend who has influenced my prayer life. Visiting her home, I see her prayer table. On it she has a Bible, a candle, flowers, slips of papers with Scripture verses on them, and pictures of people for whom she is praying. I was surprised to see a picture of the prime minister of Canada, as well as the president of the United States, on her table. Praying for the world with my friend is a soul-opening experience.

Our church prays regularly, not just for ourselves and our concerns, but for the needs of the world. We can't pray for everyone all the time, but each week it's a different group. One week we pray for those who are homeless in our community, another week it's for the conflict in Israel and Palestine. When we gather to pray, our community remembers that we are here to bring good news to the world. We are concerned about those who suffer.

There is a Benedictine monastery within driving distance of my home. When I've visited there, I have gotten up for their 3:30 a.m. prayer service. The monks there dedicate their lives to praying for the world. As we stand together in the dark, we read psalms and remind God that the world needs help. This religious community has not missed a night praying for the world in over a thousand years. Even now when I wake up at night and can't sleep, it comforts me to know that I am not praying alone. I think of those brothers at the monastery whose voices join mine in prayer to God.

Asking Hard Questions

Prayer is not just a time to share our pleasant thoughts with God. God wants to hear from us even when we are angry or upset or despairing. I am particularly struck by a passage like Psalm 109:22-25. David says that he is "gone like a shadow at evening." He says that "when [people] see me, they shake their heads." David has been waiting for God's help and it has not yet materialized. He reminds God that his situation is desperate.

David's prayers inspire me to be absolutely honest and candid with God about everything I'm experiencing. God has heard me wailing, God has heard me rejoicing, and God has heard everything in between.

I think our prayers in church can sometimes be too polite. We say everything in order and with decorum. We do well to remember that when faced with injustice and suffering, we can cry out to God: Where are you, God? We are waiting! "O Lord; let my cry come to you. Do not hide your face from me in the day of my distress" (Psalm 102:1-2).

I think our prayers in church can sometimes be too polite.

Wonderings

- Describe how different people or groups have helped you learn to pray.

- Is it easier to pray when you are experiencing good times or hard times?

- Invite people to pray in the form of questions for God.

Making Our Prayers Visible

Using old magazines, cut and paste pictures and headlines to create a visual prayer. Share about this prayer in groups of two or three.

Sing your prayers out loud: "Who Has Known the Mind of Jesus?" (*Sing the Journey* #58) or "Gentle Shepherd, Come and Lead Us" (*Hymnal: A Worship Book* #352).

TEN

Come to the Lord's Table

I am the bread of life. Whoever comes to me will never be hungry, and whoever believes in me will never be thirsty.
JOHN 6:35

God of every good gift, we seek many things.
Some of us are seeking peace,
some are seeking healing,
some are seeking answers,
and others are looking for the right questions.
We trust that you will give us what we need;
food for our deepest hunger. Amen.

Digesting the Good News

Read John 6:1-13. In the gospel of John, there is no story of an upper room where Jesus shares a meal with his disciples, breaking bread with them before he dies. Instead, this gospel writer chooses to show Jesus breaking bread in a crowd of hungry people. The next day he teaches them that he is the bread of life, and that they must eat his flesh and drink his blood (John 6:51, 53-55).

These words of Jesus are so stark and vivid that they can seem revolting. Some people found these teachings too hard (John 6:66). What does it mean that Jesus is the bread of life?

Bread was the staple food of Jesus' day, and wine was the staple drink. By comparing his body to these basic food items, Jesus uses a powerful symbol to describe how God works in our lives. Food is something we put in our mouths; we chew and swallow and it becomes something else. It becomes energy that empowers us to move and act. The actual components of the bread become part of our bodies.

Taking communion reminds us that Jesus is becoming part of us; Jesus gives us energy to live and act. Because we eat communion together, there is a mysterious unity among Christians. We are all being transformed into the body of Christ. "Because there is one bread, we who are many are one body, for we all partake of the one bread" (1 Corinthians 10:17).

Eating Together

In the society in which Jesus lived, there were big restrictions on whom one could or couldn't eat with. Purity laws and rituals were specific about what to do before eating, and it was important not to eat with anyone who was unclean. Jesus was being radical when he asked people who didn't know each other, and who were from different groups, to sit and eat together.

Later on, in the church in Corinth, there were problems around the communion meal. Some did not receive enough and were hungry (1 Corinthians 11:21). The Corinthian church included wealthy people who were likely slave owners, who were used to taking the best. And it included slaves, who had no status, who were used to getting only the leftovers. The apostle Paul wrote the church to remind them that the Lord's Supper should bring people together.

In our society today, people of different economic status and people of different races often don't rub shoulders. The church is a place where these sorts of divisions are to be overcome.

The church should be a place where anyone who is thirsty can drink, and anyone who is hungry can eat, even if they have no money.

The church should be a place where anyone who is thirsty can drink and anyone who is hungry can eat, even if they have no money (Isaiah 55:1). This is true in a symbolic way with the communion table, but it should also be true in a concrete way. The church should be a place of hospitality for hungry people.

Sometimes we spiritualize the meaning of communion so much that it doesn't have a concrete meaning. I know a congregation that always has a food bank drive on communion Sunday. The altar table has the bread and wine on it, but groceries are piled up around it. It's a strong visual symbol that communion and the body of Christ should be associated with feeding hungry people.

Waiting for Jesus

When I was in college, my friend and I had a big fight because I found her reading my diary. That Sunday, we had communion in our church, which they happened to serve around round tables. I tried to stay away from my friend in the crowd, but I arrived to find that the only open spot was at her table. I had a choice . . . would I take communion while I harbored resentment against her? Or would I choose not to take communion? Or would I forgive her? That day, the Lord helped me find forgiveness. The Lord's Supper can be a strong reconciling force in our lives.

One of the most divisive issues in the history of the Christian church has been the issue of communion: how it should be served and who can take communion. During the Protestant Reformation, reformers had strong opinions. The early Anabaptists felt that you did not have to be a priest to break the bread and serve it. They also felt that only those people who had made an adult commitment to Jesus, and were dedicating their lives to following him, should take communion.

In the Mennonite church itself, when people disagree, they have cast each other out of churches.

In the Mennonite church itself, when people disagree, they have cast each other out of churches and declared that certain people are no longer welcome at the communion table. The Lord's Table has become a place where power and politics have divided us. In my own province alone there are dozens of different Mennonite denominations because at certain points we could not bear to take communion with each other.

This is a tragedy. The very thing that Jesus gave us (his body) to make us one (by taking communion) has been the place where division happens.

Wonderings

- How could the John 6:1-13 passage about Jesus serving hungry people (and not just his own followers) change the way you look at communion services in your own church?

- Can you give examples of how your church helps to break down dividing walls between people of different classes or races?

Faith in Action

As you meet today, have communion cups and a plate as a visual symbol.

Sing "Eat This Bread" (*Hymnal: A Worship Book* #471) or "Taste and See" (*Sing the Journey* #86).

Can your church organize a food drive on the next Sunday that you serve communion?

ELEVEN

An Offering to God

Ascribe to the LORD the glory due his name;
bring an offering, and come before him.
1 CHRONICLES 16:29

Lord, with the action of offering we tell your story:
how you deal generously with us,
how you meet our needs,
how you hear our prayers,
how your goodness is from everlasting to everlasting.
Bless the offerings we give in the name of Christ. Amen.

What Shall We Offer?

Read Romans 12:1-8. Paul instructs the church in Rome to give their bodies and their minds to God. But this is not an individual enterprise, where you go to a shrine and have a spiritual experience alone with God. Spiritual worship here means connecting with something larger than yourself. It means connecting with the body of Christ, which is manifest in all the people in the church. Each member has different gifts to offer to God. Together, the church offers itself in worship to God.

Going to church and giving an offering is one of the first things I learned as a little girl. Our father gave my sisters and me each a dime before we went to church. A dime was a lot of money for a little girl—I knew exactly how much candy I could put into a little brown bag for 10 cents. I still remember the feel of the little red velvet bags that were passed around in class; we all deposited our money. This was a gift for God.

As an adult, giving a tithe can take different forms now. It can be something that is done by check a couple of times a year, or by direct deposit. For some, the symbolism of physically giving actual money is important.

Our gifts for ministry or teaching, our leadership gifts, our ability to have compassion, and our cheerfulness should all be offered to God.

Money is an important type of offering, but it is only one part, as the passage in Romans reminds us. Our gifts for ministry or teaching, our leadership gifts, our ability to have compassion, and our cheerfulness should all be offered to God.

There are many faithful givers in Scripture, but the one who comes to mind for me is Hannah. She prayed and prayed for a child, and when God gave her a son, she did not keep him for herself. Instead, she gave him as a gift to God, to serve in the temple. Samuel became one of the prophets of the Lord. Hannah's gift became a gift to the whole community.

Leave Your Gift at the Altar

In the Jewish practice of sacrifice, every gift was public. You took your lamb or turtledove and walked with it to the temple, where in front of everyone you presented it to the priest. Everyone went together to present gifts to God. In addition to offering sacrifices, people were encouraged to care for those who are poor.

Jesus was critical of people who made a big deal out of giving alms, making a show of how much they were giving (Matthew 6:2). He encouraged his followers to "not let your left hand know what your right hand is doing" (v. 3).

Mennonites in North America have taken this advice seriously. We are careful about privacy when it comes to donations. Some church traditions put commemorative plaques up in buildings to show who paid for things, but Mennonites have mostly rejected that practice. I visited one Mennonite church where they don't even pass an offering plate. They have a small brown box marked "Tithes" at the back of the church, so people can put money in it when no one is watching.

Coming from this tradition, I was surprised when, on a trip to Kenya, some churches took a very different approach to the offering. To the sound of music, people would stand up with their paper money in their raised hands and dance to the front and place it on the altar. It was so joyful; people were happy to share their offerings with God, who gives us so much.

Whatever way we are giving gifts, whether in a plate or in a box or on the altar, it is a joyful response to the God who loves us.

If You Have Not Love

Giving things to God in and of itself is not enough. We can be standing at the altar with our money in our hand, but if we remember that we have a conflict with our neighbor, Jesus tells us to go and be reconciled (Matthew 5:23-24). The money itself is not an acceptable gift when there is division in the community and we have done nothing about it.

Jesus is echoing the words of the prophets here, who continually reminded the people of Israel that God wanted them to show compassion for each other. Simply sacrificing at the temple was not enough! "I desire steadfast love and not sacrifice, the knowledge of God rather than burnt offerings" (Hosea 6:6).

Paul echoes these principles in his letter to the church at Corinth. He reminds them that you can give away all your possessions and even your body, but if you don't have love, it means nothing (1 Corinthians 13:3).

When we experience the love of Jesus, we respond by giving our lives in baptism, a lifelong commitment. We become part of the body of Christ, whose purpose is to share God's love with the world.

Wonderings

- Share an early memory of giving a gift to God. Is there someone who was significant in teaching you about giving?

- In your group, what gifts do you each bring to share with each other? If people are shy about saying what gift they offer, other people in the group can join in.

Gift Giving

Give each person in the group a small lump of modeling clay. Have everyone create a model of something that they can give to God this week. Light a candle and sing "Take My Life" (*Hymnal: A Worship Book* #389); during the singing of the hymn, individuals can place their gift on the table by the candle.

A closing prayer, "The Treasure Worth Keeping," is available from *Leading in Worship* (http://carolpenner.typepad.com/leadinginworship/2011/01/the-treasure-worth-keeping.html).

TWELVE

Serve the Lord with Gladness

*Serve the LORD with gladness: come before his presence
with singing.*
PSALM 100:2 KJV

God of grace,
we serve you in worship,
we worship you in service.
The quiet moment when we acknowledge
why we are doing what we are doing.
The deep breath when we feel like giving up,
but we don't, because this is for you.
The million little decisions we make
in the course of our lives, all for you.
The way we see the world, seeking the lost
and left behind, as you taught us.

The spoken and unspoken prayers,
shared or on our own, given to you.
Our worship service is never done,
thank God, as long as we have life
and breath to praise you.

Worship Service

Read Mark 14:3-9. In this remarkable story, Jesus says that the woman who anoints his feet has "performed a good service." She shows her great devotion, her worship of Jesus, by kneeling at his feet. He says that her actions will never be forgotten and that she has "done what she could." I think that is a great definition of worship. Worship is us doing what we can to show our love for Jesus.

When thinking of characters in the Bible who served, Mary and Martha often come to mind (Luke 10:38-42). Martha is run off her feet, and she complains to Jesus that Mary is not helping. Jesus tells Martha that simply listening is also important. I think it's important to note that Jesus never denies that

What do these two women teach us about doing what we can for Jesus?

Martha is serving. Jesus probably worked up a big appetite on his journey to their house, and I am sure he heartily enjoyed the meal Martha was preparing for him! His words highlight that Martha shouldn't judge her sister. What do these two women teach us about doing what we can for Jesus?

In everyday contexts, when we use the word *service*, we think of working for someone. Politicians are in "public service." Waitstaff are in the "service industry." It is interesting that we call our Sunday ritual of worship a service. It is our work for God. It is our task to meet together and offer thanks and praise. It is what we do as God's people.

When I worked as a pastor, I was keenly aware of how many people volunteered their service to get ready for Sunday morning. Every week, people spent hours preparing the sanctuary, practicing music, planning Sunday school, taking care of the nursery—let alone the caretaking of the building and the feeding of the people that often happened on Sundays in our church. Preparing for our communal life together is a worship service.

When I was a pastor, going to worship was part of my employment. Now that I am teaching, I again choose each week to go to church. I have to admit that, sometimes, worship even now does feel like work. I am not always excited to go to church. Sometimes I am tired and would rather sleep in. There are many other activities that I might like to do on a Sunday morning. Going to church is a sacrifice of time that I give to God.

Moment for Mission

Almost every Mennonite worship service I attend has a section for announcements. Some people like to keep announcements out of the "official" worship service and don't want to "waste" time talking about the activities of the church. I think this is a mistake. Congregations also worship God by serving the community through various programs and outreach activities.

Menno Simons, one of the early Anabaptist leaders, described what faith looks like. "True evangelical faith . . . cannot lie dormant; but manifests itself in all righteousness and works of love," he begins. Plaques have been made with excerpts or variations of this quotation. Right along with prayer and Bible study, acts of mercy are listed as ways that we live out our faith. Including reference to these acts of mercy in our worship services is only natural.

The context for encountering God in an intimate way is often not in a church building.

In my work as a pastor, I have had many occasions to talk with people about their encounters with God. The context for encountering God in an intimate way is often not in a church building. Time after time I heard of people experiencing God's presence in acts of service: helping someone stranded on the side of the road, bringing a casserole to a grieving neighbor, volunteering in an after-school program. Our true worship happens wherever we share the love of Christ.

True Evangelical Faith

There are parallels between the story of the woman washing Jesus' feet and another story about feet . . . this time the feet of the disciples. Read John 13:1-17. Footwashing was normally done by servants, the lowest of lowly jobs. Jesus specifically says, "I have set you an example."

Mennonites and a few other denominations have a tradition of footwashing as part of worship. When I've led footwashing services, it is usually on Maundy Thursday, the day we remember Jesus gathering with his disciples for that Last Supper. As I explain how we will wash each other's feet, I sense a tension in the room. People are uneasy about this ritual, because it is so extremely personal. Touching someone else's feet makes some people squeamish (even though people don't come with dirty feet). Having someone else wash your feet can feel uncomfortable.

Jesus wants us to be willing to serve each other in the most humble of ways. It reminds us of how he served people his whole life, giving his life to save us.

Wonderings

- When have you felt that worship is work? What has kept you coming?

- Have one or two people describe a footwashing service they've attended and what it meant to them.

Setting an Example

Bring a basin of water and a towel and place them in the center of your room. Invite someone to wash another person's feet while the rest of you watch. Then talk about what this practice means to you.

Sing "Jesus Took a Towel" (*Hymnal: A Worship Book* #449).

Use the prayer from *Hymnal: A Worship Book* #782 or "Maundy Thursday Confession" from *Leading in Worship* (http://carolpenner.typepad.com/leadinginworship/2011/04/maundy-thursday-confession.html).

THIRTEEN

A Blessing Service

Preparation for This Service

1. Ahead of time, gather objects that represent the work or nature of your group or anything that symbolizes what the group means to you. Arrange these objects on a table in your meeting space, with a candle in the center. Light the candle as the people arrive.

2. Print out the service, which you can download from mwusa.org/blessing-service.

3. You will need two leaders: one will read the regular print in the service, one will read the italicized print. The group can respond with the bold print.

4. If you have someone who can lead music, ask that person to prepare the hymns; if you don't have an accompanist, you will want to find recorded music to play.

5. Arrange the chairs in a circle, and place an unlit tealight candle on each chair.

Welcome

LEADER: We greet you in the name of Jesus Christ. Welcome to each one who has come—we are glad you're here! Let's join our voices to bless the Lord.

SONG: (*choose one*)
"I Sing the Mighty Power of God" (*Hymnal: A Worship Book #46*)
"Cantemos al Señor" (*Hymnal: A Worship Book #55*)
"Hamba Nathi" (Come, Walk with Us) (*Sing the Journey #2*)

Leader 1: We are here for a service of blessing. Let's begin with blessing words from Hebrews 13:20-21.

Leader 2: *Now may the God of peace, who brought back from the dead our Lord Jesus, the great shepherd of the sheep, by the blood of the eternal covenant, make you complete in everything good so that you may do his will, working among us that which is pleasing in his sight, through Jesus Christ, to whom be the glory forever and ever. Amen.*

Leader 1: We are blessed to be together today, and as a visual way of reminding us of the blessing of this group in our lives, we've brought these symbols. (*Explain what the symbols mean to you.*)

Opening Prayer

Leader 1: Let's pray together. I invite you to say the words
in bold print:

God of hope;
thank you for giving us life and breath today.
Thank you for calling us to be your children
and the many ways you bless us every day.

All: We give you thanks, Lord of life.

Leader 1: Thank you for this church where we can worship
you freely and without fear.
Thank you for giving us good news to share,
good news for all people.

All: We give you thanks, Lord of life.

Leader 1: Thank you for this group that meets for fellow-
ship and service,
and for our study of everyday worship.
Thank you for the gifts of each one,
and the love and support we offer each other.

All: We give you thanks, Lord of life.

Leader 1: Help us to join with your vision
of communities where the least are welcomed,
where those who feel lost or left behind
can take their place at the table.

All: We give you thanks, Lord of life.

Leader 1: Be with us today as we remind ourselves
of all the blessings you shower upon us,
your love flowing in and around
and through us, each and every day.

> **All: Lord of life, we worship and bless you today, and always.**

SONG: (*choose one*)

"Je louerai l'Eternal" (Praise, I Will Praise You, Lord)
  (*Hymnal: A Worship Book* #76)

"Immortal, Invisible, God Only Wise" (*Hymnal: A Worship Book* #70)

"Awake, Arise, O Sing a New Song" (*Hymnal: A Worship Book* #56)

Responsive Reading

Psalm 63:1-4 NRSV (light print) and *The Message* (bold print)

Leader 1: O God, you are my God, I seek you,
  my soul thirsts for you;
  my flesh faints for you,
    as in a dry and weary land where there is no water.

> **All: God—you're my God!**
> **I can't get enough of you!**
> **I've worked up such hunger and thirst for God,**
> **traveling across dry and weary deserts.**

Leader 1: So I have looked upon you in the sanctuary,
  beholding your power and glory.

> **All: So here I am in the place of worship, eyes open,**
> **drinking in your strength and glory.**

Leader 1: Because your steadfast love is better than life,
  my lips will praise you.

All: In your generous love I am really living at last!
My lips brim praises like fountains.

Leader 1: So I will bless you as long as I live;
I will lift up my hands and call on your name.

All: I bless you every time I take a breath;
My arms wave like banners of praise to you.

Offer another prayer, "God Above and Below," from *Leading in Worship* website.

Light of Blessing

Leader 1: The Lord bless you and keep you;
the Lord make his face to shine upon you, and be gracious to you;
the Lord lift up his countenance upon you, and give you peace.(Numbers 6:24-26)

Leader 2: *Each of you has a tealight; you are invited to light the tealight from the main candle and place it on the table for the person seated on your right. After the candle is lit, say these words to that person:* "(Name), *the Lord bless you and shine upon you.*"

(After everyone's candle is lit)

I light this candle for those who are homeless, hungry, or oppressed. Let this candle be a reminder that God cares for people who are hurting and that it is our responsibility to be a blessing to them in Jesus' name.

CLOSING SONG: (*choose one*)
"Asithi: Amen" (*Hymnal: A Worship Book* #64)
"Joyful, Joyful, We Adore Thee" (*Hymnal: A Worship Book* #71)
"The Peace of the Earth Be with You" (*Sing the Journey* #77)

BENEDICTION:

> **All: Light of the world,**
> **thank you for your blessing,**
> **which shines in us every day**
> **and even in the darkest night.**
> **Help us to be a blessing to one another**
> **and to the world.**
> **Amen.**

Leader 1: As you leave, pass the peace of Christ to one another with a handshake or a nod.

Love Feast

An alternative setting for this service is around tables as you share a simple meal of soup and bread. The candles can be at each place setting. You may want to lay out the bread in the shape of a cross. Begin the meal with the opening prayer. Offer holy hospitality to each other by serving each other. After people have eaten, share the "Light of blessing" text.

About Mennonite Women Canada

. . . a place to belong

. . . a place to connect

Mennonite Women Canada encourages women to commit to:

- nurture their life in Christ;
- acknowledge and share their gifts;
- hear and support each other;
- serve and minister across the street and around the world.

Many Mennonite churches across Canada still have organized traditional women's groups that meet weekly or monthly for the reasons listed above. We encourage women to connect with these groups or start special interest groups such as book clubs, recipe clubs, nature clubs, or peace/justice networks.

We welcome donations from all of these groups and from individuals to help us maintain our umbrella for women to empower each other as they serve and minister in ever-widening ways.

With the received donations, we

- provide scholarships for women studying master's level Anabaptist theology;

- connect women across Canada via our newsletter; a bimonthly page in the *Canadian Mennonite* magazine; a blog at http://mennowomencanada.blogspot.com/; and a Facebook page;

- support and encourage women working in Mennonite Church Canada's Witness ministries through our Pennies and Prayer Legacy Fund;

- resource women's groups with the binational, annual Bible Study Guide;

- connect with and support the provincial/area women's organizations at retreats, women's gatherings, executive meetings, and Mennonite Church Canada Assembly sessions.

Contact us at presmwcanada@gmail.com.

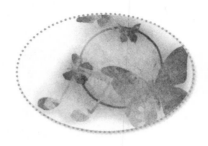

About Mennonite Women USA

Jesus said: "I am the vine, you are the branches."
JOHN 15:5

Mission statement

Our mission at Mennonite Women USA is to empower women and women's groups as we nurture our life in Christ through studying the Bible, using our gifts, hearing each other, and engaging in mission and service.

In living our mission, Mennonite Women USA

- connects globally by funding scholarships for women in church leadership training through our International Women's Fund;

- provides Sister Care seminars offering tools for personal healing, for recognizing and celebrating God's

grace in women's lives, and for responding more con-
fidently and effectively to the needs of others in their
families, congregations, and communities;

- resources women across the United States through
  leadership training events and by sponsoring an
  annual Anabaptist Bible study guide written by and
  for women;

- speaks prophetically by sharing stories of women of
  all ages and backgrounds through *Timbrel* magazine,
  the quarterly publication of Mennonite Women USA,
  and our blog, *Mennonite Women Voices.*

We'd love to tell you more about our ministry

Discover more about Mennonite Women USA programs and
events by signing up for our free monthly e-letter, Grapevine,
at MennoniteWomenUSA.org.

Mennonite Women USA
718 N. Main Street
Newton, KS 67114-1819
316-281-4396 or 866-866-2872 ext. 34396
Office@mwusa.org

About the Writer

Carol Penner lives with her husband, Eugene, in Vineland, Ontario, in a house surrounded by apricot trees. She grew up in St. Catharines, Ontario, and studied at Canadian Mennonite Bible College and Toronto School of Theology. She worked for 15 years as a pastor in Ontario and Alberta. She is currently an assistant professor of theological studies at Conrad Grebel University College in Waterloo, Ontario, where she teaches practical theology. She has a special interest in feminist theology and violence against women. She writes worship resources and shares them on her worship blog, *Leading in Worship* (leadinginworship.com). In her spare time she likes to hike on the Bruce Trail, read novels, and do anything crafty.